Life and Death
in the
Iron Age

Jennifer Foster is a free-lance archaeologist, specialising in the Iron Age. She works part-time at the Ashmolean Museum as a consultant; her recent projects include cataloguing the artefacts from Hallstatt in the Ashmolean Museum and redesigning the prehistory displays. She was previously at the British Museum and the Dept of Archaeology, Lampeter, and is currently based at the Dept of Archaeology, University of Reading as an honorary fellow. In her spare time she enjoys giving adult education lectures.

Life and Death
in the
Iron Age

Jennifer Foster

ASHMOLEAN MUSEUM, OXFORD
2002

ISBN 1 85444 179 5

British Library Cataloguing-in-publication Data
A catalogue record for this publication is available from the British Library

Front cover: Bronze terret inlaid with red and blue glass, Suffolk
Back cover: Bronze ducks which were riveted in rows around the rim of a wheeled bronze tray.
Examples of these trays are found in North Italian Villanovan graves (eighth and seventh centuries BC).
This one comes from Lezoux, France, but may have been brought from Italy in modern times (PR 329–331).

Publishing Consultant – Ian Charlton
Typeset in Columbus and designed by Geoff Green
Printed and bound in Great Britain by Grillford, Milton Keynes, 2002

UNIVERSITY OF OXFORD
ASHMOLEAN MUSEUM

Contents

What is the Iron Age?

Prehistory in Europe is divided into periods according to the tool types found by archaeologists. The later stone age or Neolithic period ended with the advent of the use of metalworking. The date varies across Europe, with the earliest copper and gold objects made from about 3000 BC; metalworking reached Britain about 2300 BC. The Iron Age is the last period of prehistory in Europe before the Roman period and lasted 7–800 years. Iron replaced bronze as the main metal used at this time. Although bronze was still used for many items such as jewellery and vessels (bowls, cauldrons and jugs), iron was the choice for blades like weapons, sickles and knives.

The European Iron Age is divided by archaeologists into two periods: the Hallstatt period (c. 800–450 BC), named after a cemetery in Austria, and the later La Tène period, named after a lakeside site in Switzerland (c. 450 BC to the Roman period). These classifications are founded on changing fashions in metalwork. In Britain, because we have few imports of metalwork from mainland Europe, the periods of the Iron Age are based on the changes in pottery and other artifacts from settlements, especially from contexts with radiocarbon dates: Early (800–400 BC), Middle (400–120 BC) and Late (120 BC–AD 43). The successful invasion of Britain by the Romans under the Emperor Claudius in AD 43 is taken as the end of the Iron Age in Britain.

People in the Iron Age lived in small settlements and farms, with occasional large settlements known as hillforts, which were defended with banks and ditches. Communities were self-sufficient, growing their own food such as grain for porridge and bread and raising sheep, cattle and pigs. Animals were kept not only for milk and meat, but had other uses as well: oxen were used to pull ploughs; cloth was made from wool; leather from hides; and bone turned into tools. Horses must have been particularly regarded because they were used only for riding or pulling light carts and chariots. Warriors would each have a horse and weapons such as a sword, dagger and spear. The fact that weapons are rarely found suggests that few men (and even fewer women) carried them.

For most of the Iron Age household goods

Years BC	Europe		Britain	
			AD 43 Roman period	
0	Roman period		Late Iron Age	
100				Wittenham sword
200	La Tène		Middle Iron Age	
300				
400				
500				
600	Hallstatt	Hallstatt cemetery	Early Iron Age	
700				Rainsborough camp
800		Bronze Age		

Fig 1: Iron Age dates in Europe

were produced by the people that used them, from local resources: houses, craft items, tools. Much of the evidence found by archaeologists consists of pottery; most was also produced locally, some at home, but by the end of the period it was mass produced by specialist potters. Special objects, such as metal and glass ornaments, vessels and weapons, came from further away. Trade around Europe was extensive, with goods such as amber, coral and salt travelling especially long distances from their source to where they have been found on archaeological sites. Goods were exchanged and bartered rather than being bought and sold, until the late Iron Age when coins were introduced. As a result of all these trading contacts, designs in art and ornament were similar across Europe, although each area had its own variations.

The Celts

The people of Iron Age Europe are often described as the Celts. The words used by Greek and Roman writers for the Celts are "Keltoi" (Greek) or "Celtae" (Latin), but these names are used in a geographical sense, as in the people from western Europe, or to describe those who spoke a Celtic language (or languages). It was a rather vague term. Britons were never described as Celts, but as "Britanni". In prehistoric Europe, people probably never thought of themselves as a large European group, the Celts, but rather as members of a tribe or small kingdom (of about 10–20,000 people). The vast majority of people would not have left their local area and probably had never travelled more than 30 km from home in their lives.

The Hallstatt cemetery

ONE OF THE MOST IMPORTANT sites in Iron Age Europe is Hallstatt, a cemetery in Austria, southeast of Salzburg on the Hallstattersee. The earlier half of the Iron Age is named after the cemetery. The earliest graves date to the late Bronze Age but most are from the early Iron Age (Hallstatt C and D), with a few being La Tène in date. Over 2000 cremation and inhumation burials have been found in the cemetery, most excavated by Georg Ramsauer, director of the Hallstatt salt mines, from 1846 to 1863. The finds in the Ashmolean were excavated after Ramsauer finished, by Joseph Stapf, the Bergmeister or foreman of the Hallstatt salt mines.

Sir John Evans and Hallstatt

The artifacts from Hallstatt in the Ashmolean Museum form part of the extensive collection of antiquities amassed by Sir John Evans and donated to the Museum in 1927 by his son, Sir Arthur Evans, the first Keeper of Antiquities. John Evans (1823–1908) was primarily a business man who owned paper mills at Hemel Hempstead, but he was also a leading scientific figure with interests in geology, numismatics and antiquities. It was he who, in 1858, finally established the antiquity of humankind to the satisfaction of the scientific community. He proved that ancient artifacts were contemporary with the bones of extinct animals by using examples from sites in the Somme Valley, France and Brixham, Devon. He wrote widely on archaeology and corresponded with the leading archaeologists of nineteenth-century Europe.

Fig 2: Map showing the position of the early Iron Age cemeteries at Hallstatt and Vače.

In 1866 John Evans took a trip to Austria with his friends Sir John and Lady Lubbock. The Hallstatt cemetery was by then famous and the men wanted to acquire a representative range of finds

Fig 3: Modern view of Hallstatt from the lake. The modern town is on the lake shore, with the Iron Age cemetery and salt mine above the trees.

Fig 4: Graves at Hallstatt excavated by Ramsauer, of two women (left and centre) and a double burial of a man and child (right). The woman on the left has a bronze belt, bracelets, necklaces and brooches.

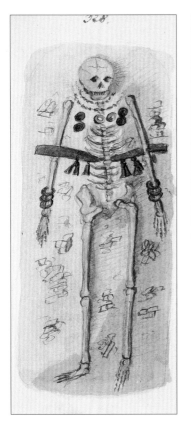

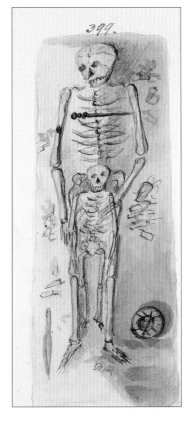

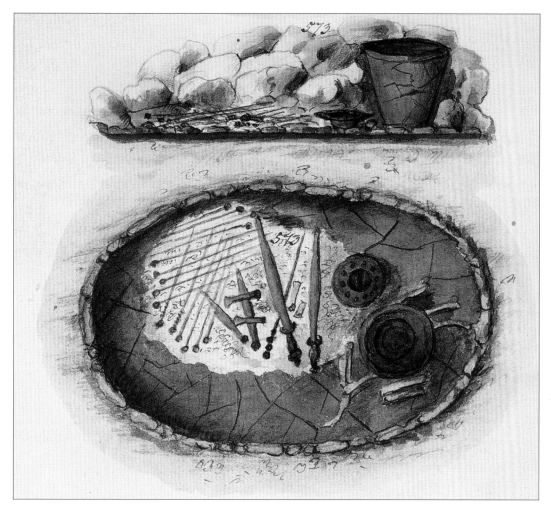

Fig 5: Cremation burial excavated by Ramsauer, of a man accompanied by bronze vessels, weapons and massive clothes pins.

from the cemetery and if possible to excavate some graves. From letters to his wife and his notebooks, we learn that Evans and Lubbock bought antiquities from Joseph Stapf, "with some things I found in a cottage down here so that we each have a more characteristic collection." They then spent two days excavating.

Letter to Fanny, Lady Evans, April 19 1866

We found the diggings too pleasant for us to be able to tear ourselves away from them. Lubbock and I breakfasted soon after 6 and about half past 7 were up at the cemetery near the Rudolfs Thurm and found that the men had already discovered a bronze bracelet and a broken fibula. I subsequently found in one of our trenches and dug out with my own hands one of the bronze socket celts with a part of the handle remaining in it and having on one part the impression of a fine twilled cloth against which it had lain. We also found no end of pottery, some iron knives, two spearheads and two bronze rings close by them, a bone pin and some small bronze studs. Lubbock found a perfect bronze bracelet and part of another and a very good double spiral brooch... Lady Lubbock was brought up to us in the course of the morning by two bearers and enjoyed the view (which is quite wonderful and unsketchable) and the quiet... The bearer brought us some bread butter eggs and wine on which we lunched and we stayed up there until at least 4 when it came on to rain.

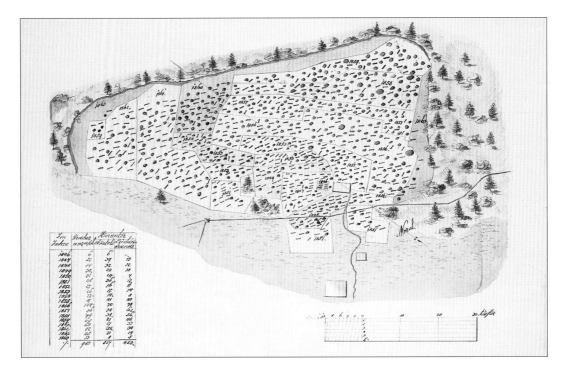

Fig 7: Plan and section of Hallstatt cemetery excavated
by Ramsauer

Fig 6: Photograph of Sir John Evans. John Evans was married three times: his first marriage to his cousin Harriet Dickinson produced five children, including Sir Arthur Evans. She died in 1858 soon after the birth of her fifth child and in 1859 John Evans married her cousin Frances Phelps (Fanny, 1826–90); they had no children. He married his third wife, Maria Lathbury, in 1892, with whom he had his daughter Dame Joan Evans, the well-known historian.

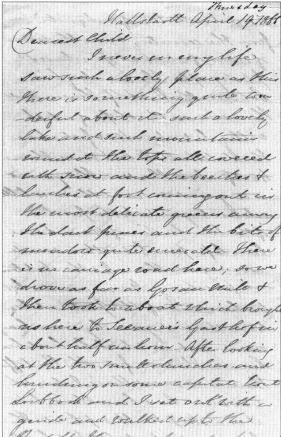

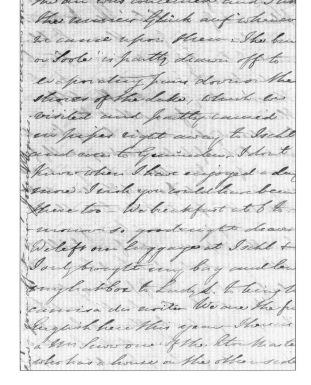

Fig 8: Letter to Lady Evans (Fanny), April 19 1866

Fig 9: This shows the modern view of the Rudolfs Thurm from the Hallstatt cemetery as mentioned in Evans' letter to Lady Evans April 19 1866:

I never in my life saw such a lovely place as this. There is something quite wonderful about it – such a lovely lake and such mountains roundabout, the tops all covered with snow and the beeches and larches at foot coming out in the most delicate greens among the dark pines and the bits of meadow quite emerald. The cemetery lies between the Rudolfs Thurm and the mine on top of a deep valley but above 1000 feet above the Hallstadt Lake and more than 4000 feet above the sea.

Evans and Lubbock were able to meet the excavator of Hallstatt, Herr Ramsauer. On leaving Hallstatt they arranged that Bergmeister Stapf would continue to excavate at their expense, and send them a range of the artifacts he found. Stapf continued to excavate and send artifacts from 1866 to 1869. Unfortunately, any excavation notes were lost along with lists of which artifacts came from which graves, so that it is not now possible to establish the grave groups. This had happened before 1916, when Lubbock's share of the artifacts was donated to the British Museum. Evan's share of the Hallstatt artefacts came to the Ashmolean Museum in 1927.

Hallstatt grave goods

The importance of the Hallstatt cemetery lies in Ramsauer's detailed recording of the contents of the individual graves. This recording allows a wide range of finds to be dated in relation to each other. Grave goods are dated by seriation. An early grave for example, may have a bronze axe and sword (dating to the late Bronze Age), so a dress pin in that grave is likely to be early. Another grave may have an iron socketed axe and an iron knife, with another type of dress pin which is likely to be later. Other graves can then be dated on the type of dress pin that they contain. In the same way finds from

Dates BC	Hallstatt salt mines	Phases of the Hallstatt cemetery	Dating of the Iron Age by Reinecke (the German archaeologist)
400	Salt mine continues to c400 BC	Cemetery ends c 400 BC La Tène	
450			Ha D
500			
	Early Iron Age	Ha 2	
550			
	mine continues		
600			
			Ha C
650			
		Ha 1	
700			
	East mine starts 731 BC*		Ha B
750			
	North mine worked		
800	Late Bronze Age	Urnfield	

Fig 10: Dates at Hallstatt

other sites can be dated by reference to Hallstatt. In using this technique heirlooms may pose a problem, and not all types change over time. Spiral brooches, for example, were used throughout the life of the cemetery.

The salt mine started in the late Bronze Age (the Urnfield period, named after the burial custom of putting the cremated bones in urns, in cemeteries) and a few cremation graves date from that period. Four objects in the John Evans collection are of this date. Most of the other dated grave goods are from the first phase of the cemetery (Hallstatt 1: 730–650 BC), with fewer from Hallstatt 2 (650–475 BC) and only three objects from the succeeding La Tène period (from 475 BC).

Fig 11: Modern view showing the position of the Hallstatt graves on the steep slope. Today there is an archaeological trail on this site.

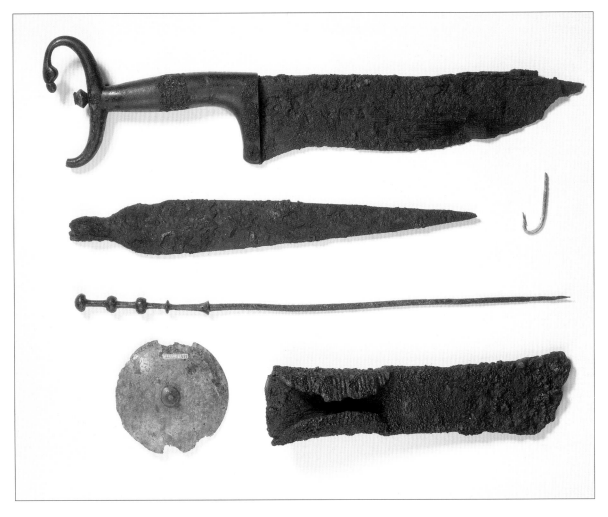

Fig 12: Objects associated with male graves at Hallstatt were large clothes pins, weapons such as swords and spears, tools such as axes, knives and fishhooks, and belt plates. Men also wore a few beads and rings. Some graves contained buckets or dishes.

Life styles at Hallstatt

The wealth of the Hallstatt community was based on the salt mines (salt is still extracted there today). Salt was an important item in the past, both for food but also for use in many industrial processes such as dyeing cloth and metal production. The cemetery lies on the steep slopes of the mountain valley, with the Iron Age salt mines further up the valley.

Unfortunately the settlement at Hallstatt which would have been associated with the cemetery has not been located (it was probably close to the salt mines, but was covered by a landslide c. 400 BC). It is possible, however, to reconstruct the lives of the inhabitants from their burials. There were both cremation and inhumation burials at Hallstatt. The bones were left in the graves after excavation and

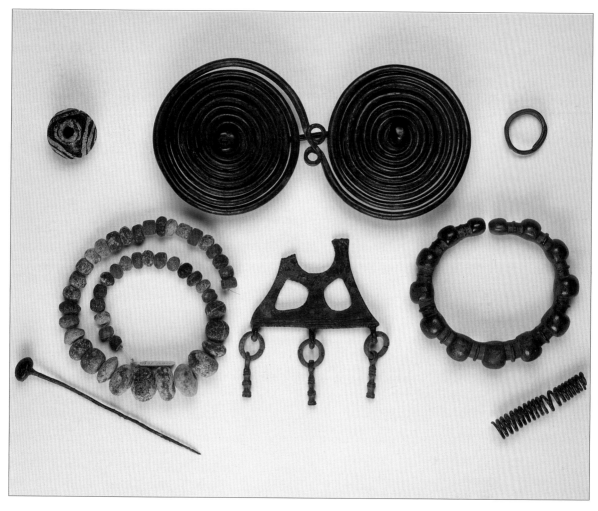

Fig 13: Female graves at Hallstatt contained brooches, glass and amber beads, jangle pendants, bracelets, rings and hair decorations.

subsequently decayed. As a result, we have no information from Hallstatt about the age at which people died or the diseases they suffered from.

Letter to Lady Evans, April 19 1866:

The ground is very uneven and there is little external guide to the position of the tombs. Two of them have been left open but with a wooden covering over them but the skeletons are perishing. It was curious to see how one of the parties ribs were stained green by some bronze ornament in which he had been buried.

However, subsequent excavations of early Iron Age burials where the bones were preserved and studied have shown that it is possible to distinguish between male and female graves, because men and women were buried with distinct objects. Men were buried with weapons and tools, and their clothes were held on with pins. Women were buried with jewellery, hairpins and gold objects, and their clothes were fastened with brooches. Both men and women had knives, metal containers and metal belts (see reconstruction, page 00). Of the graves excavated by Ramsauer, 488 were prob-ably women's graves, while only 296 can be assigned to men. However, about 76 graves cannot be assigned (some had no grave goods), so perhaps these were also male graves. This is probably because men were more likely than women to be buried without distinctive grave goods.

Vače: an early Iron Age cemetery in Slovenia

THE EARLY IRON AGE CEMETERY at Vače in Slovenia contained over a thousand graves, dating to the same period as the Hallstatt cemetery. The contents from a small group of graves excavated by Duchess Paul Friedrich of Mecklenburg in 1905–7 and 1913 are in the Ashmolean Museum. They were well-recorded and the finds are still in their grave groups: thirteen individual cremation graves (flat graves), and

Fig 14: Diagram to show the division of grave goods from burials at Vače into male and female types.

Grave	Bronze vessel	Belt plates	Iron spear	Iron Axe	Iron knife	Bracelet (2+)	Bracelet	Bead 4+	Bead (1-4)	brooch	Fingerring/ earring	Needles	Spindle Whorl	Jangle pendant	Bones	Male/ Female
BII2							X									?
BII3			X	X							X					?
BII5					X											?
BIV1										X						?
F1										X						?
F5										X						?
F7										X						?
F8										X						?
F10										X						?
F12				X					X	X	X				X	?
F13	X															?
BII1				X		X		X		X					child	child
BI2						X		X		X				X		F
BIII2										X	X					F
BIII4					X					X						F
BIII5					X											F
BIII8				X									X			F
BIII9						X	X									F
F3												X				F
F4						X		X		X		X				F
F6							X									F
F9						X				X				X		F
BI3	X			X												M
BIII1		X	X	X			X		X							M
BIII6			X	X											male	M
BIII7	X		X	X			X			X						M

B=Barrow F=Flat grave

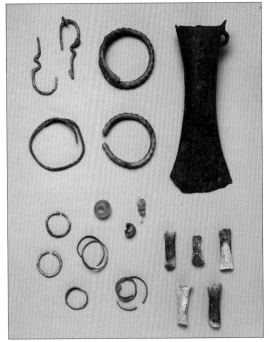

Fig 15: These are the contents of the grave of a child, from Barrow II, Grave 1 at Vače. The contents are surprising as they combine both traditional male and female grave goods; an axe would normally be from a man's grave, and bracelets and beads from a woman's grave, while here they are together in the same grave. The jewellery is very small so probably belonged to the child, but it is impossible to say whether it was a boy or a girl because, although the bones survived, skeletons cannot be sexed unless the person has reached adolescence.

Fig 16: Rich graves of the Hallstatt period contained bronze vessels. This large bronze bucket from Vače (Barrow I, Grave 3) is decorated with a frieze of eight animals (possibly goats or deer) with foliage in their mouths, followed by a man in a cloak, with a staff, possibly a shepherd. The decoration is known as the Situla style and is typical of central Europe, occurring particularly on bronze buckets (situlae). There are two styles, one centred on Este in Italy, the other in Slovenia to which this bucket belongs. The style began in the late sixth century and continued into the fourth century BC.

eighteen burials under four mounds (Barrows). Their gender or wealth (great or little) made no difference to the way the people from Vače were buried; just as many women were buried under barrows as men, and there were also child burials. However, as at Hallstatt, the men were buried with tools and weapons, and the women with necklaces, needles and brooches. Rich graves contained numerous objects, such as lavish ornaments (one woman had twenty-two bracelets) and unusual or imported objects such as metal vessels. Archaeolo-gists have difficulty interpreting these grave goods. Were these people the richest members of society? Were the people buried with just one pot and a brooch poorer or were they of a different status, or age? Were the objects designed to accompany the dead to the other life, or were they objects used in the person's life? There may have been a taboo on using objects belonging to the dead. Often they look like personal items: they are well-used, rather than made just for the burial.

Economy and trade

VALUABLE ITEMS AND MATERIALS were traded over long distances (even if in relatively small amounts) during the Iron Age, though usually in a series of short steps between local centres along the trade-routes. Rivers must have been important in transporting goods, though before modern times many had lots of rapids. Wagons, carts and pack-animals were also used. Salt, for instance, was traded over long distances, from mines in Austria or from the coasts of Europe. In Britain salt was produced by evaporation from seawater, especially on the Essex coast, and from salt beds at Droitwich, Worcestershire, and in Cheshire. Pottery containers for salt (known as 'briquetage') from Droitwich are found as far afield as the Thames valley. Trade in salt brought local prosperity to places which could supply it.

During most of the Iron Age the economy was probably based on barter exchange. Metals such as gold, silver, bronze and iron would have been high value items, as were items that had to travel long distances. Many people would have worn their wealth in the Iron Age, in the form of necklaces and bracelets, so they could display how much they owned. Amber from the Baltic Sea was traded across the whole of Europe, a thriving trade during the Bronze Age, which continued into the early Iron Age. Amber is a fossilised resin probably prized for its orange colour, but also for its unusual properties: it floats on water, is always warm and has static attraction. The Ancient Greeks called it elektron, from which we get the word "electricity".

A monetary economy was introduced in north-western Europe at the end of the Iron Age. Gold

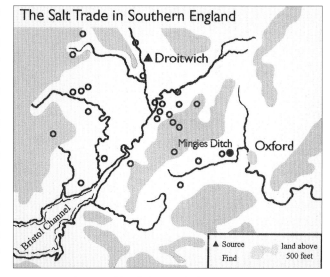

Fig 17: Distribution of the findspots of salt containers from Droitwich, Worcs. The salt was exported in these pots.

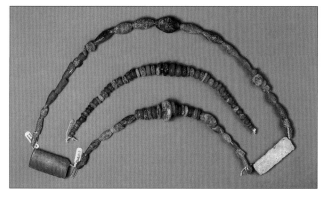

Fig 18: Amber necklace from a grave at Hallstatt, Austria.

Fig 19: Gold coin (stater) of the Dobunni tribe. Most Celtic coins had a face on one side and a horse on the other. This horse has a triple stranded tail.

Fig 20: Iron bars known as currency bars are known from late Iron Age contexts throughout southern Britain. The iron was of known quality, with the ends of the bars forged to show how good the iron was. Currency bars were not tools, but iron stock, ready to be turned into tools. Sword-shaped currency bars were of high phosphorus iron, spit-shaped bars were low-phosphorus, so that the blacksmith could select the type of iron for the tool to be made. These bars, from a hoard of 147 found at Salmonsbury Camp, Bourton-on-the-Water, could be used in barter, in exchange for other goods, or made into iron objects.

They use as money gold or bronze coin or iron bars gauged to a standard weight

Julius Caesar (c. 54BC) *Gallic Wars*

coins first started to be used as a result of contact with the Greeks who used coinage. The first coins found in Britain, from c. 200 BC onwards, are the same as coins found in France: of gold with a face on the front side (obverse) and a horse on the other (reverse). Most coins were imported into Britain from France, but a few were probably minted in Britain.

The function of these early coins is unknown. They were made of high value gold, and were worth far more than would be needed for everyday payments. Perhaps they were used as gifts to nobles or their followers, or to pay mercenaries for a year's work, or to store as wealth. They were literally worth their weight in gold.

After 50 BC bronze and silver coins were introduced in France and Britain, which were of lower value and were probably used as currency or money to buy goods. They would still be worth much more than modern coins. These coins are inscribed with the names of tribal rulers using the Latin script.

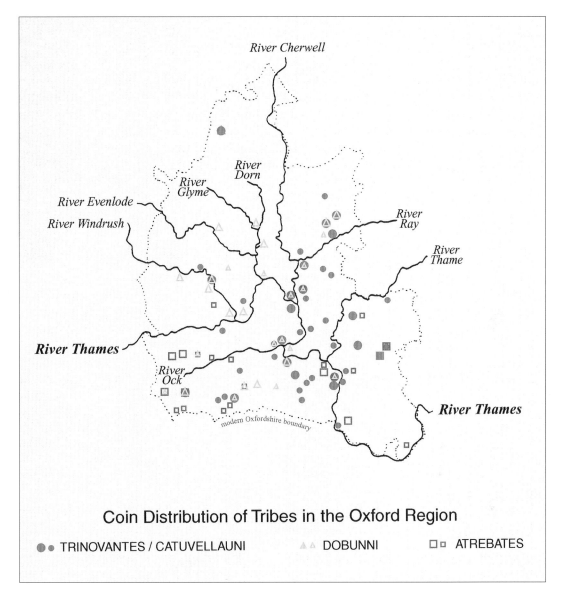

Coin Distribution of Tribes in the Oxford Region

● ● TRINOVANTES / CATUVELLAUNI ▲ ▲ DOBUNNI ☐ ▫ ATREBATES

Fig 21: Coins were produced by each tribe to be used
within their tribal area. Coins from the Oxford region
are mainly those of the Catuvellauni (minted at St
Albans), the Trinovantes (from Colchester) and the
Dobunni (minted at Bagendon). South of the Thames are
the coins of the Atrebates (minted at Silchester), which
are rarely found in this area. Information for this figure
was kindly supplied by Dr. Philip de Jersey.

Food

CEREALS PROBABLY FORMED A MAJOR part of the Iron Age diet; in Britain, spelt wheat and barley were the main crops, with a little rye and oats growing as weeds. Peas and beans were also grown, along with vegetables, such as *Chenopodium album* (Fat Hen), a plant now thought of as a weed. Most meals were probably a type of porridge or vegetable stew of peas, beans and grains with herbs, with roasted or boiled meat. People also ate unleavened bread cooked in clay ovens. Wild foods such as blackberries, mushrooms and nuts would have been collected, but formed a small proportion of the diet. We know about Iron Age food from remains of meals, such as bones and seeds, left on archaeological sites, and particularly from the study of stomach contents of bodies preserved in bogs in northwest Europe.

Grain was ground by hand on quern stones, which was a very time consuming job. At the beginning of the Iron Age these were flat stones (saddle querns): later two-piece querns were introduced, with one stone which turned round on top of the lower one. The utensils used for preparing food, cooking beside an open fire and serving were made of pottery. Sometimes remains of meals are found burnt onto the inside of pots. Most pots in

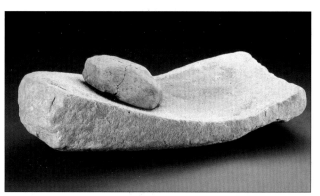

Fig 22: Saddle quern with grinding stone from an Iron Age farm at Mingies Ditch in the Thames Valley.

Fig 23: Both spoons (of wood, bone and horn) and iron knives are known from Iron Age contexts, though not forks. This large iron knife with remains of a wooden sheath is probably from Sopron, Hungary.

Fig 24: Honey was very important in the past as it was the only sweetener. It was used in cooking and making mead (a sweet alcoholic drink) and the honeycomb wax was used in bronze casting. This seems to be a jar for serving honey or pickles; it dates from the sixth century BC and is from Guben, Poland.

The lower classes drink wheat beer prepared with honey, but most people drink it plain. It is called corma. They use a common cup, drinking a little at a time, not more than a mouthful, but they do it rather frequently.

Athenaeus, quoting Posidonius about the people of France in the Iron Age.

Fig 25: Most Iron Age pots were multipurpose, for cooking and eating. However, some pots were obviously made for one purpose only: perforated bases are for straining (perhaps for making cheese), while very large pots were probably used for storing dry foods, such as grain, flour, fruit or vegetables. They might also have been used for making beer or, when cracked, for storing clothes as there is very little evidence for furniture in the Iron Age. All these pots are from Oxfordshire and date to the Iron Age.

the Iron Age were multi-purpose, with no pottery plates known in Iron Age Europe except in areas of Roman influence. Wooden platters were possibly used, but have not survived. However, wooden buckets were available for carrying water and beer, and wooden tankards for drinking from, while bronze cauldrons were also used for cooking, suspended over the fire.

These are two contemporary quotes about the food of people living in Iron Age France.

The country produces lots of grain and millet and nuts, and all kinds of livestock.   Strabo

Their food consists of a small number of loaves together with a huge amount of meat, either boiled or roasted on charcoal or on spits. Any part that is hard to tear off they cut through with a small dagger which hangs from their sword-sheath in its own scabbard.   Athenaeus

Domestic Animals

Food animals

Almost all animal bones (about 95%) found on Iron Age settlements come from domesticated animals, mainly sheep, cattle and pig, with a few horses and dogs also represented. There is very little evidence from Britain that horses and dogs were eaten, though they were occasionally skinned. Very few wild animals seem to have been hunted in Iron Age Britain: the occasional deer for meat and antlers,

Fig 26: Animals commonly used for decoration were cattle and pigs (or wild boar). It is interesting that sheep are rare, though they were an important source of meat; possibly the animals used in decoration were valued for their fierceness and courage, or their importance in myth, rather than their economic importance. It is not always possible to identify the animal. This picture shows two bulls, one possibly from Hungary, the other, lacking one hoof, from Britain and a boar from Gower Cave, Rhossilly, south Wales.

Fig 27: Horse and rider on a ceremonial wheeled bronze sculpture from Strettweg, Austria, from a replica in the Ashmolean Museum. The wheels go round so that it could have been wheeled along, though not steered. It was put into a cremation burial in the seventh century BC. The cremated bones were in a bronze pot on a stand (probably originally used for washing hands). Also in the grave were an iron axe, a spear, bridle bits and pieces of horse harness, a person's belt, and pottery.

Fig 28: Archaeological examples of cart fittings and harness: bronze rein-rings (terrets) to guide the reins on a cart, iron and bronze bridle bits; and linchpins used to hold the wheel onto the cart or chariot and an iron pin used to hold pieces of the cart together.

In chariot fighting the Britons begin by driving all over the field hurling javelins, and generally the terror inspired by the horses and the noise of the wheels are sufficient to throw their opponents' ranks into disorder. Then, after making their way between the squadrons of their own cavalry, they jump down from the chariots and engage on foot. ...Thus they combine the mobility of cavalry with the staying power of infantry.

Caesar, Gallic War V,1

and animals like otter, beaver and badger for their fur. Occasionally bird bones are found indicating that birds such as ducks were also eaten. But fish bones have been found on very few Iron Age sites in Britain, even on the coast; it is possible that people did not eat fish, even though they had the technology. Perhaps there was a taboo on eating fish, or they were cooked so thoroughly that the bones do not survive. Another possibility is that fish may have been skinned and boned where they were caught, and the bones thrown away, leaving no evidence to survive on archaeological sites.

Milk would have been important in Iron Age Europe, though few specialised processing tools survive. However, recently chemists analysed the burnt remains on the inside of a pot from Scotland and found that it was from milk or a milk product such as cheese. Cattle bones are found on most sites in Britain, and are usually from older females and castrated males (oxen), which suggests a milk-based economy, rather than cattle being reared for meat. Sheep were kept mainly for wool and possibly milk, with both young males and elderly females being eaten. Pigs were mainly kept for meat. The bones of Iron Age pigs are very similar to wild boar and they may have run wild part of the time.

Animals used as decoration

Images of animals were used in the Iron Age to decorate objects such as pendants, belts, brooches and rings. Depictions of birds, especially ducks, were common in the early Iron Age.

Horses

Horses were prestige animals in the Iron Age, kept for riding and pulling light two-wheeled carts (chariots). Larger wagons would be drawn by oxen, as horses could not pull heavy weights until the horse collar was invented in the Medieval period. Horse bones are sometimes found in strange contexts, such as pit burials or even in their own graves in cemeteries. Evidence for riding horses, and the carts and chariots used in the Iron Age, is provided by depictions used as decoration and the remains of harness; bridle bits, lynch pins (to hold on the wheels), terrets (rings for the reins to pass through), strap unions (for joining pieces of the leather harness) and other cart fittings.

Crafts and production

Tools

IN THE EARLIEST PART OF THE IRON Age bronze was still the main metal used for making tools, but iron rapidly took over as the period progressed. Many metal tools are familiar to us today; agricultural tools such as plough-shares and sickles, and carpentry and metalworking tools, like saws, chisels and hammers. Multi-purpose knives were for cooking, chopping and carving; and shears for shearing sheep and also for cutting hair, leather and even sheet metal. Axes were the common tool and were presumably used for wood-

working and chopping firewood – essential jobs when all food was cooked over an open fire. Bone and antler were also used in the past for many objects such as handles, and tools such as needles, chisels, awls and modelling tools. Experiments have shown that it is possible to cut through wood with a bone chisel, though many bone tools were probably used for leather working.

Pottery

Pottery in Europe was handmade at the beginning of the Iron Age but by the La Tène period the use of the potter's wheel had been copied in places from the Greeks and Etruscans. In Britain pots were still handmade using coils of clay until about 50 BC. Pottery was at first made in the settlement where it was used, some by the people who would use it and some by specialists who travelled from place to place. As techniques became more complicated, pottery was produced in manufacturing centres and traded to settlements. Surprisingly, the most specialist pots are the ones that look the crudest: the large storage jars which are more difficult to produce than the small decorated 'fine wares'. Homemade pots would be fired at a low temperature in uncontrolled firing conditions in a bonfire. Fillers (or temper) such as grog (ground-up old pottery), stone or shell were added to the clay to prevent the pot exploding when it was heated, in firing and cooking.

The technology to make wheel-made pottery was introduced into Britain in the first century BC. Wheel-made pottery was already being used in

Fig 29: Selection of Iron Age tools: early Iron Age bronze axe with the handle held on by the bent-over wings; later iron axe, with the handle fitted into the socket; iron shears; knife with a bone handle; bone awl and needle.

France; the earliest wheel-made pots were imported, but quickly British potters copied the new technology. Pots thrown on a wheel had a more regular look.

Throughout most of the Iron Age in Britain pottery was made by hand, using coils of clay. For technical reasons, fillers varied through time: in the Oxford area flint or quartzite was used in the late Bronze Age, shell in the early Iron Age, sand in the middle Iron Age and grog in the late Iron Age. Some pottery is beautifully decorated, incised in geometric or curving patterns, and sometimes with white infill, or more roughly with fingerprints or finger nail marks.

Many other containers would have been made of wood or leather, which survive only in exceptional archaeological circumstances. More common are metal fittings, such as the metal handles and binding hoops from buckets or tankards. Many sophisticated carpentry techniques were in use by the Iron Age, such as carving, lathe-turning, and the building of buckets and barrels with staves dowelled together.

Fig 30: Late Iron Age stands and firebars from a kiln at Long Hanborough. Towards the end of the Iron Age British pots were fired in kilns, resulting in hard-fired, regular pots. The unfired pots would be balanced on top of the bars and a fire lit underneath.

Working with textiles

Textiles were produced at home in the Iron Age. The first stage was spinning. Woollen or linen threads were spun by hand using a wooden spindle and spindle whorls of clay, stone or even bone. A very few rich graves in France and Germany contain silk, probably imported from India or China, but cotton was not known in Europe until after the Roman period. The threads were dyed in a variety of natural colours obtained from plants, lichens and minerals and were then woven into colourful checks and stripes. Iron Age weavers were highly skilled, making cloth of different weaves. Cloth rarely survives in archaeological contexts, although impressions in clay or in the corrosion products of bronze and iron survive.

Glassworking

European Iron Age glass workers were specialists working on only a few sites. They used a range of beautiful colours, which they could combine to make multi-coloured beads of contrasting colours. The beads were spun while the glass was hot,

Fig 31: (left) A very unusual glass whorl from a grave at Hallstatt, Austria. Exceptionally, its wooden spindle also survived.

Fig 32: (right) Impression of a very fine textile in mud from a grave at Vače, Slovenia. Length of fragment 12 mm.

Fig 33: Textiles were woven on upright looms, with the vertical warp threads kept taut by weights hanging at the bottom. These weights could be made of clay, stone or chalk.

Fig 34: Glass was used for objects such as bracelets and beads.

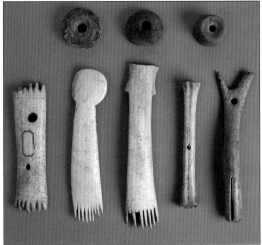

Fig 35: Spinning and weaving equipment is common on Iron Age settlement sites. Spindle whorls were used with wooden spindles to spin the thread. Antler weaving combs were used to press up the weft threads and keep the fabric tight. Many were decorated and have a hole or notch, so that they could hang from a line close to the loom or from the weaver's belt. Also shown are a shuttle and loom-fitting, both made of bone.s

rather than being made in moulds. Decoration in a contrasting colour, such as a trail or circle, was added to the surface and then the bead was rolled to push the decoration into the surface. In general, glass working was restricted to beads and other small objects, although in mainland Europe bangles were also made. Glass was imported into Britain and was obviously in short supply. It was used only to make small objects, such as beads and gaming counters. From the third century BC British bronze objects were decorated with red glass studs; by the first century AD coloured inlays (red, blue and yellow) were common, often made from re-cycled pieces of glass.

Metalworking

Iron working

IRON CAME INTO WIDESPREAD USE during the Iron Age, but not because it was more useful than bronze. In fact, early iron was not a harder or stronger metal and iron could not be melted like bronze and poured into moulds. All iron objects had to be produced by heating the metal and hammering it into shape. However, iron ores are widely available throughout Britain and Europe unlike copper, tin and lead ores. When late Bronze Age trade routes across Europe were disrupted leading to a shortage of bronze, iron started to be used.

Iron first appears in Britain about 750 BC, but iron objects were rare until the third century BC. Iron production was small and the technology was unsophisticated. From about 400 BC smiths started to use different types of iron for different jobs. Phosphorus iron is hard but brittle – adzes, large sickles and ploughshares were made of this. Swords and daggers were made of low-phosphorus softer iron; it is better to fight with a sword that bends and loses its edge rather than shatters! Steel (harder carbon-rich iron) was not widely known in Europe until the Roman conquest, though smiths were able to harden the edges of tools.

The tools used by the Iron Age blacksmiths are rarely found, but are very similar to those used up to the present day: hammers, tongs, chisels, files and anvils.

Bronze working

Bronze continued to be used for many objects in the Iron Age and standards of bronze working continued to improve until the introduction of new techniques by the Romans.

Bronze is a mixture (alloy) of copper and tin, with lead sometimes added to help it flow into a mould. Other metals used in the Iron Age were gold and silver. Brass (an alloy of copper and zinc) was introduced into Britain late in the first century BC.

Sheet metal

Large bronze objects were made from sheet metal, while smaller objects were cast.

Sheet bronze vessels such as buckets, bowls and jugs were prestige items in the Iron Age, probably associated with drinking alcohol: beer, mead and, in the late Iron Age, imported wine. The vessels were made from beaten sheets of bronze. In the early Iron Age objects were made from several sheets riveted together, with bronze studs pushed through a hole in the sheet and beaten flat, while later entire vessels were hammered from one sheet of bronze. To prevent cracking while making sheet bronze, or working it into objects, the bronze had to be heated after every six or so strokes of the hammer. The additional details such as handles were attached with solder or rivets. Finally all the tool marks on the vessels were smoothed away by polishing.

Fig 36: A pair of cast spoons, with cast decoration from an Iron Age site at Penbryn, Ceredigion, Wales. One spoon has three circles, the other two circles on each side. There are about ten pairs of ritual spoons of this type known in Britain. Typically, one spoon has a hole, the other is divided into four areas, with metal inlays in three, gold, silver (missing here), and bronze. They were possibly used for divining (telling the future), with liquid dripped from the upper spoon through the hole onto the lower spoon.

Fig 37: (right) Cast bronze rein ring (terret) inlaid with red and blue glass. Terrets were attached to the yoke of a chariot and the reins of the ponies passed through them.

Casting

Small objects were cast by melting the metal in small crucibles and pouring it into clay moulds. These moulds would be broken to get the object out and then thrown away. As casting became more expert, decoration was often cast onto the object.

Applied decoration

Decoration was usually applied to metal objects after manufacture. One of the easiest techniques was repoussé or embossing, where a design was beaten from behind, leaving a raised pattern on the surface. Other methods of decoration were engraving, or punched decoration using a shaped punch or inlay with coloured glass.

Ornament and appearance

P EOPLE IN THE IRON AGE WERE FOND of personal decoration. Men, women and children wore beads and bracelets, and held their clothes together with flamboyant pins and brooches.

In the Iron Age there were no buttons and

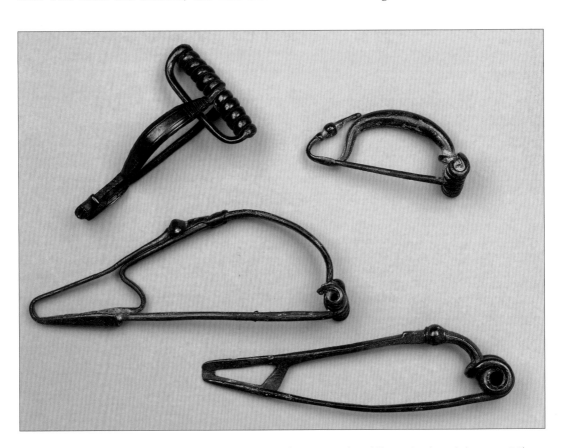

Fig 38: Early Iron Age brooch with animal's head on the foot (Hallstatt D, 600–500 BC); early La Tène brooch (450–200 BC); middle La Tène brooch (250–100 BC); and late La Tène brooch (100 BC-Roman conquest).

Fig 40: Reconstructions of people from Hallstatt (see above, page 12), wearing and using the fine objects that they owned in their lifetimes. Most people at Hallstatt were buried with pots, possibly originally with food inside, and were dressed in their clothes. Men were buried with weapons and tools, and their clothes were held on with pins. Women were buried with jewellery, hairpins and gold objects, and their clothes were fastened with spiral brooches. Both men and women had knives, metal containers and metal belts.
Painted by Helen Ganly.

clothes were attached with pins and belts.

From the fifth century BC brooches were used. At first they were made of one piece of metal, usually bronze, bent into a safety pin shape, while later brooches were made with separate pins. Some were very elaborate or joined in pairs with a chain. Clothes were made of brightly coloured cloth, sometimes with bronze or silver sequins sewn on, and both men and women wore belts decorated with bronze.

Neckrings (or torcs), which were first used in the Bronze Age, continued in use in the Iron Age. The richest people wore gold torcs, but silver, bronze and even iron torcs are common. Torc and bracelet sets are sometimes found in burials. Necklaces of beads, glass, bone and amber are mostly found in women's graves, but were occasionally worn by men. Rings were usually made of a simple piece of bronze wire bent into a circle, worn as finger or toe-rings. They were worn by all, one or

Fig 39: Torcs from Ulceby, Lincs made of electrum
(a mixture of gold and silver)

two per person. Earrings rarely survive, because they were made of thin bronze or silver wire. They were made for pierced ears.

Mirrors were introduced in the Iron Age, copied from Etruscan (Italian) designs. They were of polished bronze; recent experiments show that the image is very clear if the mirror is polished enough. The back of a mirror plate was decorated with curving designs, which would be seen when it was held up. Mirrors are found in female graves, though only rich women would have owned a mirror. Both men and women were interested in their appearance. Men shaved with small bronze razors (and later iron ones) and cut their hair and beard with shears.

Weapons and Warfare

WEAPONS ARE LESS COMMON IN THE Iron Age than in the Bronze Age, although large scale fighting is recorded by Julius Caesar and other Roman and Greek authors. Warfare consisted of intertribal fighting and from the fourth century BC battles against Greek and Roman forces, or as mercenaries for them. The northern peoples fought as foot soldiers, but they were renowned as cavalry. The main weapon in the Iron Age was the spear, while in battle warriors would also carry a sword, worn on the right hip. From the end of the third century BC sword blades were longer than 80 cm, at least 20 cm longer than the Roman sword. Most warriors would have been protected in battle by a leather or fabric helmet and a wooden or leather shield. These rarely survive, though the metal fittings

Fig 41: Miniature models of weapons: bronze shield, from Leafield, Oxon and a bronze shield and a sword from a late Iron Age shrine at Frilford, Berks.

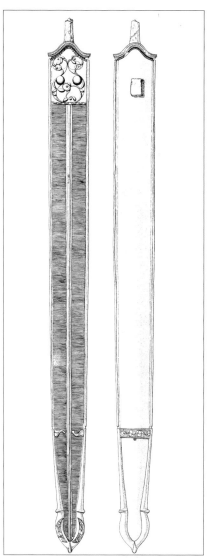

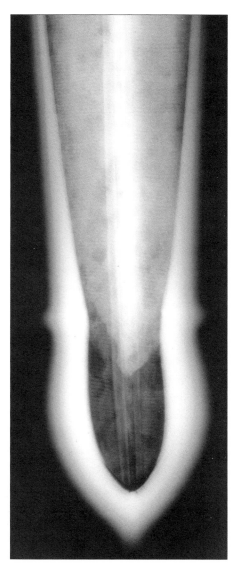

Fig 42: (left) The Wittenham sword is a good example of a late Iron Age iron sword in a bronze scabbard (c100 BC). It was found in the River Thames at Little Wittenham, Oxon. The scabbard is made up of two beaten bronze plates overlapping at the sides, held on at the tip by the scabbard end, known as a chape. On the back is a loop through which the belt was threaded when it was worn.

Fig 43: (middle) Illustration of the Wittenham sword

Fig 44: (right) X-rays of the Wittenham sword show that the sword inside the scabbard is of typical late Iron Age shape, long, pointed and flat in section. The blade stops 47mm from the end of the scabbard. This scabbard may have been made for another sword, but the hilt end fits perfectly. Perhaps the end of the sword was damaged and it was re-forged.

are fairly common. Some elaborately-decorated bronze shields are known from the Iron Age, such as those found in the River Witham and the River Thames at Battersea; these are of thin bronze sheet and would have been no use in battle and were probably for display only. Bronze helmets are also rare and may also have been for show.

Some objects that appear to be weapons, such as knives, spears, daggers and arrowheads, may have been used in hunting. Many burials contain knives with blades along one edge or daggers (two-edged knives) but it is not clear how they were used in fighting, if at all. Some, for example, are from women's graves. Because of the nature of the archaeological record in the Iron Age, most weapons come from burials, with a few fragments from settlement sites where they were probably lost. Some weapons have been found on ritual sites such as temples, while many, such as the Wittenham sword, have been dredged from rivers, where they were probably thrown as ritual deposits. Sometimes miniatures were used, like shields, swords and axes; these are interpreted as ritual objects, rather than toys, because most are found in shrines.

Their armour includes man-sized shields, each decorated individually. Their trumpets are of a peculiar barbaric kind; they blow into them and produce harsh sounds which suit the tumult of war. Some wear suits of iron chain-armour, while others fight naked. Instead of the short (Roman) sword they wear long swords held by iron or bronze chains and hanging down their right leg. The spears which they carry in battle have long iron heads.

Diodorus Siculus, writing about the
Iron Age tribes in France.

Fig 45: Spears were the main weapons carried into battle. The Iron Age spearheads had long wooden shafts with the heads of bronze (in the earliest Iron Age), iron or bone. Many spearheads were long and heavy but, despite this, they were thrown in battle rather than used for stabbing.

The Oxfordshire Region

Hillforts

THE HILLFORTS IN THE OXFORD region are typical of such sites in Britain and across Europe, large settlements surrounded by one or more ramparts and ditches. Some hillforts began as unenclosed settlements in the late Bronze Age. Within the defences was a community of perhaps 60–100 people, living in round houses, with four-post granaries and storage pits for seed grain.

Because of the impressive defences, hillforts appear to be primarily defensive sites in a troubled

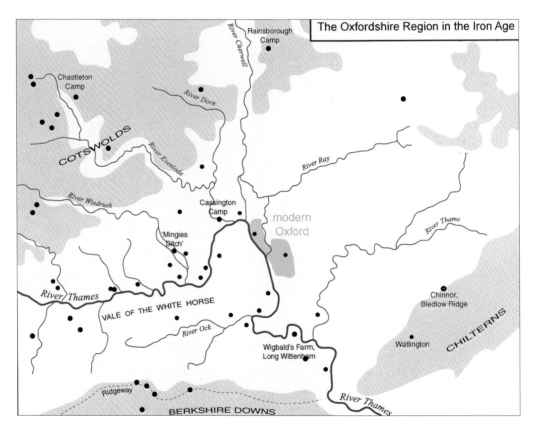

Fig 46: Iron Age sites in the Oxford region.

landscape. On many sites piles of clay slingshot have been found presumably for defending the hillfort. Experiments have shown that they can be accurate as weapons even at 200m. However, the bank and ditch systems may be for purposes other than defence, for example to protect animal stock and food supplies from thieves and raiders. Perhaps they were to keep out wild animals such as wolves or bears, although the landscape of Iron Age Britain was open and farmed, similar to today and wild boar is likely to have been the fiercest animal around. On many sites the defences are over-elaborate for raiding and a determined raider would be able to force a way in, though perhaps getting out would be more of a problem. Recent work in the Cotswolds and Upper Thames Basin has shown a network of undefended farms, which would have made easier targets than hillforts. The ramparts on many sites were spectacular, and may have been mainly for display, to funnel the visitor through an imposing entranceway.

Because of the spectacular look of hillforts, and the effort needed to make the ramparts, it has been suggested that they were administrative or market centres, or the homes of chiefs. However, the

Fig 47: Aerial photograph of Uffington Castle hillfort taken by Major Allen, showing the hillfort and the famous white horse cut into the hillside beside it. The horse probably predates the hillfort, which was occupied from the seventh century BC. The hillfort may have been unused in the later Iron Age, but there was Roman activity on the site. There is a series of hillforts along the Berkshire Downs, following the line of the ancient track of the Ridgeway; a section of the track next to Uffington Castle has been excavated and was certainly in use in the Iron Age.

objects found in them are similar to those from smaller, poorer sites: craft objects, home made pottery and food debris. If these are the homes of chieftains, they had the same standard of living as everyone else.

The hillforts in the Oxford region are on the areas of high ground: in the north Rainsborough Camp and Chastleton Camp are on the Cotswold Hills, while in the south there is a series of hillforts along the chalk hills of the Berkshire Downs: Rams Hill, Uffington Castle, Hardwell Camp, Segsbury Camp and Blewburton Hill, with Wittenham

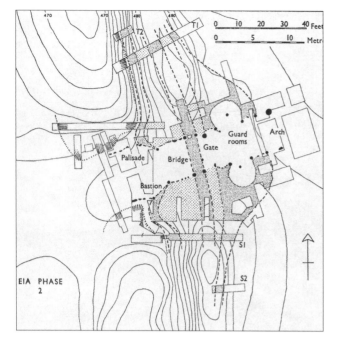

Fig 48: Guard chambers at Rainsborough, seventh to sixth centuries BC

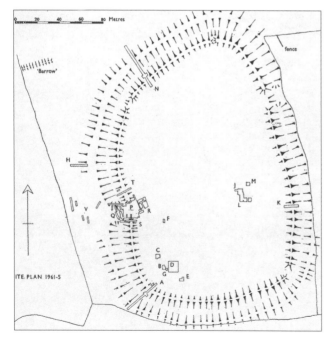

Fig 49: Rainsborough from the air

Clumps on an outlying chalk outcrop. Other features of the Iron Age landscape were field systems, many of which survived on the Berkshire Downs into the twentieth century: small square fields each of about 2 acres, outlined with banks which were probably hedged in the Iron Age. Some sections of the landscape were divided with long sections of bank and ditch, many called Grim's Ditch. There is a section on the Berkshire Downs, another from the Thames east from Wallingford, and a third circular bank in north Oxfordshire.

Rainsborough is a large hillfort with two ramparts and one entrance. Excavations from 1961–5 showed two major phases of use, with abandonment in between. In the first phase, during the seventh to sixth century BC, the inner rampart was faced with stone and circular stone-walled guardrooms were constructed at the entrance. There were large impressive timber gates, with a bridge across the entrance. This phase came to a violent end, when the wooden structures at the entrance were destroyed by fire. After 200 years the ramparts were rebuilt of earth.

Objects from the site show the usual range of domestic artifacts: pottery, weaving equipment, bone and antler working and food preparation. Some of the weaving and spinning equipment was found on the floors of the guard rooms, probably from the time when the hillfort was abandoned, unless the guards whiled their time away by weaving! There were no weapons, but a few clay sling shots suggest how the hillfort was protected from attack. Pottery was handmade locally, much of it probably by the people in the hillfort. The pots were baggy, without distinctive features and crudely finished with little decoration.

Farms

Hillforts are few and far between, but scattered over the Iron Age landscape every few kilometres were small farms, of about one to four houses, with associated fields and trackways. In the Oxford region, sheep were mainly raised on the upland sites (as they get foot rot in wet conditions), and cattle and horses in the lower-lying Thames Valley (on the rich pasture). These lowland sites would exchange butter, cheese and horses for wool and corn.

Fig 50: Reconstruction of an Iron Age house at Butser, Hants. British houses were circular, unlike those on the continent, which were rectangular.

Mingies Ditch, Hardwick, Oxon

Typical of the small settlements in the Oxford region are Mingies Ditch and Watkins Farm in the valley of the Thames. Mingies Ditch was a small farming settlement dating from the fourth to second centuries BC. It was a circular ditched enclosure containing one or two houses and four-post storage buildings at any one time. Another outer enclosure was probably for stock. Both ditches had hedges inside. About six adults plus children probably lived on the farm.

The settlement took advantage of lush grazing to raise dairy cattle and horses. At any one time there were probably ten cattle, ten horses, twelve sheep and goats, a dog and pig on the farm. This very high proportion of horses suggests they were being reared on the site. Most of the horses were older than ten years at death, so foals were probably sold. Sheep were killed either at 8–9 months (for meat) or 5 years (so were kept for wool

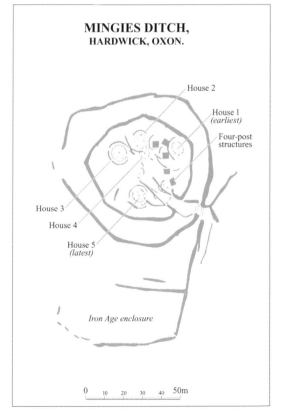

Fig 51: Plan of Mingies Ditch and Watkins Farm, Oxon. (After Allen and Robinson 1993)

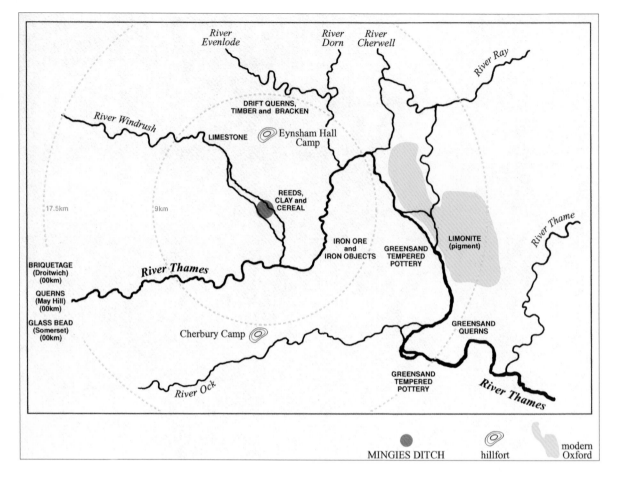

Fig 52: Resources at Mingies Ditch. (After Allen and Robinson 1993)

production and possibly milk). Most cattle were older females, which suggests they were kept for dairying.

Saddle querns for grinding grain, and finds of carbonised grain, show that cereals (spelt wheat, barley and rye) were a major part of the diet, but they were probably grown at other nearby sites on the terraces. Some wild foods were used, as shown by finds of blackberry pips, but wild animals do not seem to have been eaten. Despite being on the river, no fish bones have been found, suggesting that the people here do not seem to have eaten fish.

Resources at Mingies Ditch

Most of the materials used at this site came from the local area. The round houses were made of wood with cob (mud) walls and thatched roofs (probably reed). Floors and tracks were covered with locally quarried gravel and burnt limestone (probably originally used for cooking, or parching grain). The inhabitants repaired bronze items themselves and had a few locally made iron tools. Most pottery was made on site. However, even this poverty-stricken family had a few objects from far away: querns of May Hill sandstone came from Gloucestershire, salt in pottery containers from Droitwich and a glass bead from Somerset. Altogether this was a well-functioning and self-sufficient farm.

Cassington, Oxon

This is a settlement dating to 300–100 BC, excavated in the 1930s. At that time houses were rarely recognised by excavators, so the material from this site comes from drainage ditches and storage pits that were used for rubbish disposal. Animal bones show that the inhabitants were making use of cattle, sheep and pig, with a few dog bones. Pottery consisted of homemade jars and bowls, some of which were decorated with incised loops. Clay was also used in house construction, daubed onto the wattle structure of the walls and as mud floors. Tools such as awls and needles were made from red deer antler and bone, while some fragments of metalworking debris (a mould for bronze casting and some iron forging slag) suggest that the people here were mending small bronze and iron objects. An iron sickle and the iron binding loop and handle from a bucket are among the few metal implements to survive; most metal objects would be recycled once they wore out.

Fig 53: Objects from Cassington, Oxon

Burial in Britain

Burial in the early to middle Iron Age in Britain

WHILE THERE WERE EXTENSIVE IRON Age cemeteries on the mainland of Europe, burials are rare in Britain, except in a few areas such as Yorkshire and the south-west. Many Iron Age settlements in Britain contain a few burials in pits and ditches, but far too few to account for all of the people who would have lived on the sites. The explanation for this 'absence of burial' could be that archaeologists have not found the places where these people were buried, but alternatively that their bodies may have been treated in a different way from traditional burial or cremation. One suggestion is that the bodies were first exposed to the elements, and then some were buried. At Danebury in Hampshire excavations have shown that, while there were some twenty-five "normal" burials, many more bodies seem to have been exposed. Some time after the deaths of the individuals, selected parts of the bodies, such as pelvises, skulls or, in the case of children, the upper half of the body, were buried in pits within the hillfort. These body parts were still articulated. One of the interesting questions is: if most people were treated after death in this alternative fashion, why were some people buried in what we would now consider to be a normal way?

A similar case was found at Watkins Farm, Northmoor, Oxon, where five groups of human bones were found. One was the burial of a woman, aged 30, in a waterlogged pit with a board of alder wood (possibly a gaming board) and a leather object, but the body was not complete and beetle evidence showed that she had been buried probably five months after death, perhaps after exposure. Many other British Iron Age sites have parts of human skeletons in pits and ditches. This may seem macabre, but difference in burial ritual may not mean that the dead were treated without reverence.

Burial in the late Iron Age in Britain

In the late Iron Age there was a change in funerary fashion in south-east England. Burials once again appear in the archaeological record, with large organised cremation cemeteries becoming widely used. In these cemeteries each cremation burial was in an individual pit, often placed in rows, laid out with grave goods such as a brooch. The fashion for cremation spread to Oxfordshire just before the Roman conquest. For example, there is a cremation burial of a woman in a small circular grave from Watlington, c1–50 AD. A locally made butt beaker dating to the Claudio-Neronian period (AD 41–68) contained the cremation and a bronze Colchester brooch, which may have been placed on the corpse for the funeral. Another butt beaker contained a chalk or soapstone bead, possibly strung on a bronze wire earring, and fragments of an iron knife. Also in the grave were a plate and bowl. All the pottery was wheel made.

Fig 54: Grave goods from a late Iron Age woman's grave at Watlington, Oxon.

Glossary

Artifact: an object that has been used by people. It may have been made (eg a pot), or modified (a stone tool) or used (a hammerstone).

Awl: sharp pointed tool for making holes. There are many bone awls from the Iron Age.

Bridle bit: metal bar that goes into a horse or pony's mouth. The bit is attached to the leather reins and the rider controls the horse by guiding the reins. Iron Age bridle bits were usually made in several sections, so they were flexible.

Briquetage: pottery container for salt in which the salt was transported.

Bronze Age: period of prehistory in Europe that followed the Neolithic stone age. The period started about 2500 BC in mainland Europe and about 2300 BC in Britain. Copper, bronze and gold were worked in this period, though people also used stone, bone and organic artifacts.

Bronze: a mixture (alloy) of copper and tin, with lead sometimes added to help it flow into a mould.

Clothes pin: before the use of buttons and zips, clothes were held together with ties, belts and brooches, or with metal or bone pins. Some Iron Age clothes pins were very large (30 cm long).

Grave group: Prehistoric people generally placed objects in graves along with the dead person: pots, food remains and personal items. A grave group is a group of objects associated together in one grave.

Hallstatt: a cemetery and salt mine in Austria dating to the early Iron Age (800-450 BC), after which the first phase of the Iron Age is named.

Hillfort: a settlement, usually for over 100 people, with rampart(s) and a defended entrance. They were usually on hilltops, and are typical of the Iron Age.

Iron Age: The Iron Age is the last period of prehistory in Europe before the Roman period and lasted from about 800-0 BC. Iron replaced bronze as the main metal used at this time.

La Tène: a site in Switzerland in Lake Neuchatel, where hundreds of metal objects, particularly swords, were found in the nineteenth century. The La Tène period (the second phase of the Iron Age, c450-0 BC) is named after this site

Linen: material made from fibres of the flax plant.

Loomweights: Iron Age weaving looms were upright, with weights at the bottom to keep the warp threads taut. The weights were circular or triangular and made of stone or pottery.

Lynch pin: metal bar used to hold on the wheels onto a cart or chariot.

Oxen: castrated male cattle, used for pulling carts and ploughs.

Quern: a large stone used for grinding, usually grain. Until the later Iron Age, these were dished stones called saddle querns. In the late Iron Age, rotary querns were used: one stone grinding over the top of another. They were turned by hand using a handle.

Rampart: defensive bank usually with an outer ditch, around an Iron Age settlement. Sometimes they had walls or a wooden parapet on top.

Ritual: an object or action that is not mundane or ordinary. It may be associated with religion, or the supernatural.

Scabbard: container for a sword, which hangs from

a belt. In the Iron Age scabbards were of leather or bronze plates, held together with binding.

Settlement: an archaeological term for a domestic site where people lived, containing houses, storage buildings and evidence of daily life.

Spindle whorls: were used with wooden spindles to spin yarn.

Strap union: a decorative bronze for joining pieces of the leather harness on a pony/horse, similar to horse brasses used today. In the Iron Age buckles had not been invented.

Terret: rings fixed to a cart or chariot for the reins to pass through. Usually made of bronze or iron.

Urn: pot used for the burial of cremated bones.

Weaving combs: were used in weaving fabric to press up the weft threads and keep the fabric tight. Many were decorated and have a hole or notch, so that they could hang from a line close to the loom or from the weaver's belt.

Illustrations

Further Reading

Allen, TG and Robinson, MA (eds) 1993 *The Prehistoric landscape and Iron Age enclosed settlement at Mingies Ditch, Hardwick-with-Yelford, Oxon* (Oxford Archaeological Unit).

Audouze, F and Buchsenschutz, O 1991 *Towns, villages and countryside of Celtic Europe* (Batsford).

Briggs, G, Cook, J and Rowley, T 1986 *The Archaeology of the Oxford Region* (Oxford Univ Dept for External Studies).

Cunliffe, BW 1983 *Danebury* (Batsford).

Cunliffe, BW 1991 *Iron Age Communities in Britain* (Routledge and Kegan Paul).

Cunliffe, BW 1995 *Iron Age Britain* (English Heritage).

Dyer, J 1985 *Hillforts of England and Wales* (Shire Archaeology no 16).

James, S 1993 *Exploring the World of the Celts* (British Museum Publications).

Megaw, R and V 1986 *Early Celtic Art* (Shire Archaeology no 38).

Ritchie, WF and Ritchie JNG 1985 *Celtic Warriors* (Shire Archaeology no 41).

Stead, IM 1996 *Celtic Art* (British Museum Publications).

Acknowledgements

I HAVE RECEIVED UNLIMITED HELP from staff and volunteers at the Ashmolean Museum, without whom this book would not have been written. Most of the photographs were produced by the Photographic Department of the Ashmolean, many taken specially for this publication by Nick Pollard, Jane Inskipp, Anne Holly and David Gowers. Fig 40 was painted by Helen Ganly while she was Artist in Residence in the museum. I am very grateful to Keith Bennett and Graeme Campbell for the line drawings, maps and other illustrations (Figs 2, 17, 21, 43, 46, 47, 48, 51 and 52). Martin Bell kindly supplied the site views (Figs 3, 9, and fig 50 is my own). Julie Clements helped with access to the archive and liased with the photographic department. I appreciate the support given by Ian Charlton and Roger Morey. I am indebted to colleagues who read a draft of this book and made many valuable comments, particularly Alison Roberts, Mansel Spratling and Rachel John. Lastly I would like to thank Angela Cox for her sterling support throughout.